THE COMPLETE GUIDE

YOUR AUTOMATED BUDGET

You will live at peace knowing your financial values and responsibilities are being funded each month without you even having to think about them!

MANAGE YOUR MONEY ON AUTOPILOT
WITH SYSTEMS THAT WORK FOR YOU

ERIC HUDSON

YourAutomatedBudget.com

Copyright © 2024 Your Automated Budget

YourAutomatedBudget.com All rights reserved.

You are welcome to print a copy of this document for your personal use. However, no part of this publication may be reproduced, stored, or transmitted in any form or by any means, electronic, mechanical, photocopying, recording, scanning, or otherwise, without the prior written permission of the author.

Limitation of liability/disclaimer of warranty: While the publisher and author have used their best efforts in preparing this e-book, they make no representations or warranties regarding the accuracy or completeness of the contents of this document.

The advice and strategies contained herein may not be suitable for your situation. You should consult with a professional where appropriate. Neither the publisher nor the author shall be liable for any loss of profit or any other commercial damages, including but not limited to special, incidental, consequential, or other damages.

Due to the dynamic nature of the Internet, certain links and website information contained in this publication may have changed. The author and publisher make no representations of the current accuracy of the web information shared.

Table of Contents

Acknowledgments v

The Mission Of This Book vi

About Me vii

Preface xii

Chapter 1 Getting Started, First Things First 1

Chapter 2 Holding Account 7

Chapter 3 Fixed Account 15

Chapter 4 Irregular Expenses Account 25

Chapter 5 Everyday Expenses Account 33

Chapter 6 Freedom Accounts 40

Chapter 7 The How-To 43

Chapter 8 Emergency Fund 55

Chapter 9 Paying Yourself First 58

Chapter 10 The Wrap-Up 62

ACKNOWLEDGMENTS

It's safe to say that a project like this doesn't get accomplished alone. I'm eternally grateful to my family for supporting and enduring me through this process.

To my family, Vanessa, Savannah, John-David and Callum, you're the reason I live.

A big thank you to Jeremiah and Monique McLean for the opportunity and for pushing me to step out and do something like this. I would never have had the courage on my own.

Finally, I would like to thank God for His grace in my life. I am rescued daily because of Him.

THE MISSION OF THIS BOOK

I am sure you are like me. You want to do well with the financial resources you have been given.

The mission of this book is to teach you how to do it automatically.

I will show you how to prioritize and schedule your cash flow so your family's money goals and priorities are met every month, guaranteed. You will live at peace knowing your financial values and responsibilities are being funded automatically each month. Then, the fun begins, as you are free to enjoy what you have earned without guilt because the important things have already been paid automatically. How can this happen? Well, my friend, you'll have to read further...

ABOUT ME

ERIC HUDSON,
STRATEGIC WEALTH COACH

To say I was born in a rural area is an understatement. Our house was surrounded on three sides by pastureland and on the back by a pond and woods. Our town didn't even have a red light.

We weren't completely living in the dark ages; we did have a caution light. Boom!

I'm unaware of anyone in my family having ever earned a four-year college degree. During my high school years, college was never brought up in conversation within my family, at least that I can remember. I ended up attending a little technical college and received an Associate Degree in Electronics Engineering.

It is very popular in our culture today to encourage kids to find what they're passionate about and pursue those passions to find a suitable career. That was not the case where and when I grew up. What you were good at or what you liked never really came into the conversation.

Your requirement, as a young man at least, was to find a job, work hard, and do whatever it took to provide for your family, even if you were miserable for 40 years. You were allowed to have fun at night or on the weekends, but work had only one purpose, and that was to provide for your family.

It wasn't until much later in life that I learned to pursue my passions. I began working for a company in 2004, where the leadership challenged me to do just that. They allowed me to become a financial counselor and begin helping people get out of debt, save, etc.

During this time, I learned that I had a passion for understanding money, how it works, and how to help people reach their goals and gain peace in their financial lives. After becoming a financial counselor, we really worked hard to follow a monthly budgeting plan. Unfortunately, we realized we couldn't stick with it.

We could do it for a while, but then we would fall back into bad habits. It was frustrating because we really wanted to do it. I understood how important it was, but we couldn't seem to pull it off. Here I am, a financial counselor espousing the importance of a monthly budget, but behind the scenes, we couldn't pull it off ourselves.

It was defeating, embarrassing, and frustrating. I knew there had to be another way to get budget-like results without having to do a budget every month, another way to manage our finances month to month, week to week and day to day. I had to find a new way.

Somewhere around this time, I read a book called "The Automatic Millionaire" by David Bach. The premise of this book was that you could become wealthy if you "paid yourself first." The magic of it was to pay yourself first automatically.

Now, what does it mean to pay yourself first? Most of us approach saving money by telling ourselves that at the end of the month if there's any money left after we've paid our bills, we will save that money. The problem is that there's never any money left.

Something always happens, or we always find somewhere to spend the money. The premise of "The Automatic Millionaire" was to decide how much you want to save each month, whether that be a percentage or a fixed amount and have that come out of your check before anything else.

Then, have those dollars deposited into a retirement or investment account. In other words, pay yourself first. Additionally, the transfer should happen automatically. Then, adjust your lifestyle to live off what is left.

Bach's idea made total sense to me and sparked an idea of my own. What if you could automate all or almost all your financial decisions? What if you could predetermine where your money went before you got your hands on it? Could this happen, and could this idea work?

This idea would not have worked when Vanessa and I were first married in 1990. There wasn't any such thing as mobile banking.

But in 2005, this looked like it could be a real possibility. So, I decided to try it. I decided I would try to take Dave Ramsey's cash envelope system and automate it, using multiple accounts and debit cards.

You are reading this book today because it worked!

Admittedly, it was a little rough and clumsy at first, but now, I would not live any other way. And here is the good news

I'm going to show you how to do it step-by-step. Are you ready?

Let's change your life!

PREFACE

Before we get started, I feel I should stop here and give a piece of advice to those of you who have a home-based business or business of any kind. You should have a business-only bank account for business-only transactions.

The salary you withdraw from your business account is a business expense, but when you deposit it into your personal account, it becomes your family's income. You should never pay for personal expenses with money from your business account. Transfer money from your business account into your personal account first, and then pay your bills from that account.

Here is an example. Let's say you need to go grocery shopping, but you do not have enough money in your personal checking account to make the purchase. You will need to pull the money from your business account as salary (business expense) and deposit it into your personal checking account (family income).

Now, use the money from your personal account to purchase the groceries. This method is best because you can deduct business expenses at tax time. If you do not have a business account or if you have muddied the business account by using it for personal expenses, then it becomes challenging to remember which expenses were business-related and which were personal.

This could cost you money. If you overpay your tax bill because you did not count all your legitimate business expenses or count things as business expenses that are not, you could end up on the wrong side of an audit. Just trust me and keep them separate.

ARE YOU **READY** FOR LASTING **CHANGE?**

CHAPTER 1

GETTING STARTED
FIRST THINGS FIRST

First, if you are married or if you share income and expenses with someone in your household, this system is designed to bring you closer through mutual agreement and understanding in managing your finances.

If you make the decision alone without having your significant other on board, this system will not work as it should.

I think it is important enough to bribe, beg, or plead for your partner to join you.

Do whatever you must to get your partner on board, and preferably read through this book with you to get an understanding of what it is you want to do.

> *This system works best when there is agreement*

GET YOUR PARTNER ONBOARD

See if you can find common ground. Ask them if they agree that you could do better with money as a team by saving more, giving more, paying off debt, etc.

If you can get a "yes" answer to that question, then explain that what you want to set up is a system that is easy to understand, transparent, and will give you budget-like results without the need for a monthly budget.

Committing to this system does take a little planning, but after that, it really runs itself. Not only that but every month, there will be guilt-free money in your accounts to spend however you want, without any questions or judgement.

In fact, you and your significant other will cheer each other on no matter how the money is spent!

Second, Read the entire book prior to setting up any of the accounts. Don't feel as though you need to open each account as you are reading the chapter on that account.

Chapter Seven will review each account and spell out how to set the system up.

Third, you will open several checking accounts at your bank. This system works best when all the accounts are at the same bank and have these parameters.

ACCOUNT PARAMETERS

1. Free Checking Accounts (if your bank charges you for a checking account, it may be time to change banks).
2. Unlimited transactions - this usually is not a problem for checking accounts.
3. Minimum Balance Requirement—The account should have a very low or no minimum balance requirement. You will be spending many of the accounts down to a very low dollar amount every month.
4. Electronic Access - App (phone) and computer access is a must.

On the next page you will see the Your Automated Budget Flowchart. We will refer back to this as we walk through the program. You may want to bookmark the page with the flowchart.

Don't worry if the flowchart and boxes don't make sense to you yet, they will as you read through the book.

At the end of this book, I will walk you through opening accounts with your bank. I'm not having you do that now because this plan is customizable to your financial situation. I want you to read this book and work through the program, but I want you to work in the spirit of the book and not necessarily do it exactly the way I do it.

Make it yours. This plan is designed to create peace in your life, not another set of dogmatic rules for you to follow. OK, let's look at the Flowchart.

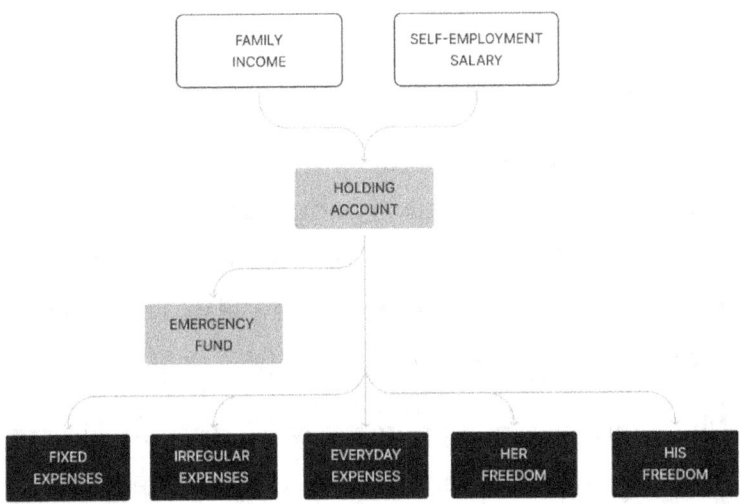

WHAT QUALIFIES AS FAMILY INCOME AND SELF-EMPLOYMENT SALARY?

What I mean by this is all the streams of income from all the jobs you and your partner have that are for your personal use/expenses. I am specific here because the way we are going to use this system is for personal budgeting use.

For those of you who have a home-based business or are self-employed, your income would not be the gross amount your business generates each month. Your income would be what you have decided to withdraw from that business as a salary.

The white boxes represent all the salaries you receive from any source. For example, let's say you are self-employed, and your business generated $10,000 in total top-line revenue last month.

Ideally, some portion of that revenue would be brought into your personal budget to use for personal expenses, let's say $2,000. That $2,000 salary is what the white boxes represent. They also represent a traditional work-for-pay situation (W2 or 1099).

Whatever your bring-home pay is, that is what the white boxes represent. Those white boxes do not represent bank accounts. All the gray or black boxes on this flowchart represent bank accounts.

CHAPTER 2

HOLDING ACCOUNT

Let's start at the top. The Holding Account's job is to gather all your personal income streams and automatically distribute them to your other accounts as directed.

All your salary or personal income streams should come into the Holding Account first, and this should happen via direct deposit if possible.

The Holding Account is a checking account. There will be no debit card access to this account.

You might ask why it is important to have a Holding Account. Why can't you allow your money to be direct deposited into one of the other accounts and then disburse from there?

Great question. The answer is simple.

Eventually, I want you to have a month's salary or enough to cover a month's worth of expenses sitting in the Holding Account, waiting until the 1st of the month before it disburses to the other accounts.

I realize that for many of you, that can't happen immediately, and that's okay. But at some point, the real magic happens when you transfer all the budget for the month from the Holding Account into separate accounts on the 1st of the month.

It makes everything much cleaner. Then, while you are working through and living that month, all your income, whether you are paid weekly, bi-weekly or monthly, builds up in the Holding Account, waiting for the first of the next month. Then, the process starts all over again. It is a clean way to manage your monthly budget. Work hard toward this. You will thank me later.

Here's an example. Let's imagine that all your income for January equals $10,000. It does not matter if that is from one salary or many streams of income. That

$10,000 should sit in the Holding Account waiting on the 1st day of February.

Then, on the 1st of February, you will have your bank automatically transfer the appropriate amount to each of the other accounts that we will discuss later. Again, this will be an automatic recurring transfer. Meaning after you set it up once, it will happen automatically.

You will rarely have to think about it again until something changes in your financial life and you need to make a small tweak to the automatic fund transfer.

We should pause here and discuss your bank's fund transfer feature. Every bank I have encountered has a feature built into its online or app platform that allows you to automatically move money (fund transfer) from one account to another on a recurring basis.

You should be able to choose 4 specific parameters:

1. When to move the money.
2. How much to move.
3. What account to move the money to.
4. The ability to make the transfers recurring.

We will make all these transfers recurring, meaning the very same thing will happen every month without us having to do anything.

If your bank does not have an automatic fund transfer option, it is time to get on your horse, ride over to the bank and tell them you want your money. It is time to change banks.

Until you can save for a month's worth of expenses in the Holding Account and have it waiting for the upcoming month, the process would look like this: Let's say you are paid on the 1st and 15th of each month.

Both of those deposits should come directly into the Holding Account (direct deposit if possible).

Then, based on your situation and how you set it up, this money will immediately and automatically be disbursed to the other accounts as needed. Don't worry if you don't quite understand how it works yet.

You will over the next couple of chapters. Remember, you will set this money movement to happen automatically. After a few months, you won't even have to think about it.

HERE IS HOW YOU DO IT.

Once all your accounts have been opened you will access your online banking and tell it when, where, and how much money to transfer from the Holding Account to the other accounts.

> *Literally, assign your bank's software the task of automatically moving a specific dollar amount on specific dates to specific accounts. Ideally, this automatic transfer should happen once a month, on the first day of the month.*

I know for some of you, giving up that kind of control makes you a little queasy, but believe me, this is life changing! I have been doing this for years, and I have never had even one mistake made by my bank's software. Oh, there have been mistakes, but when I researched the mistakes, it was me!

For those of you who cannot quite let a salary for a whole month build up into the Holding Account waiting on the 1st, we can still work the plan. Here is how that might work.

Let's look at an example of you getting paid on the 1st and the 15th, $5,000 on the 1st and $5,000 on the 15th, each month for a total of $10,000 per month.

Your salary of $5k on the 1st would go into the Holding Account. Then, on the 2nd, you would have your bank's software automatically move the appropriate amount into the other accounts that we will discuss later.

Similarly, when you get paid on the 15th into the Holding Account on the 16th, you would have your bank's software automatically move the appropriate amount into the other accounts that we will discuss in the next chapters.

> **Again, all this money transfer will be automatic and recurring. So, you will set it once and forget it until something changes that requires you to tweak it.**

Your situation might be such that your income is not the same every month. In other words, some months you have plenty of money to cover expenses, but the next month, your income does not quite cover expenses.

This scenario works better within the system than what you are currently, likely, doing. Let's say you need $10,000 every month to cover all your budget/expenses. We will assume January is a good month, and your income is $10,200. So, $10,200 goes into the Holding Account during January, waiting until February 1st to be disbursed.

However, since you only need $10,000 to cover your expenses, only $10,000 is automatically transferred out of the Holding Account and into the other accounts to cover your February expenses. The additional $200 that you did not need in February sits in the Holding Account, waiting on the month that you are short.

Let's say your February income is S9,800. Only $9,800 is deposited into the Holding Account, which is $200 short of the $10,000 you need to meet the March budget.

Well, now you have $200 left in the Holding Account from January's higher salary. So, on March 1, $10,000 is automatically transferred to the other accounts to cover March expenses. Easy.

See what we just did there? Be honest. Right now, when that good month comes, you spend it all and then when the bad months come, you are left scrambling. Maybe you are using credit cards to make up the difference.

Well, my friend, those days are gone! You are getting better already, and we have only just begun!

> **Helpful Tip:** I do recommend having some "cushion" in all the accounts we will be discussing, wherever possible. Maybe that is $50 or $500... whatever you are comfortable with. I would not take any account down to $0 every month unless it were an absolute necessity. There could be a penalty associated with a $0 balance.

Something to think about... If you find that after running this system for 6 months to a year, you have money built up in the Holding Account, then consider increasing your savings or investing. The Holding Account is not a savings account or Emergency Fund account; its job is only to hold and move money.

CHAPTER 3

FIXED ACCOUNT
NO DEBIT CARD ACCOUNT

Oh, the Magic! This account is such a beautiful thing.

The purpose of this account is to create peace in your life by eliminating the possibility that you could accidentally or impulsively spend money that was supposed to pay your house payment, car payment, life insurance premiums or any other important fixed expense.

We do this by moving money earmarked for those expenses into the Fixed Account, which has no debit card or check access!

> *Create peace in your life by eliminating the possibility that you could overspend.*

The Fixed Account removes any possibility of a spending mistake! In my budget, I actually call this account my "**All The Good**" account. Why? Because primarily in this account, I make my money do all the good things I want it to do, and it all happens automatically. Let's see how it works.

This account is for all your expenses that are a fixed dollar amount and have a fixed payment date. This includes things like your mortgage, car payment or possibly charitable contributions.

The fixed account should pay for every expense with a fixed date and amount, whether monthly, annually, or anything in between.

Maybe you have some credit card debt that you are determined to get rid of, and you want to spend $500 a month on it until it is gone. I would use the Fixed Account to pay that expense.

For simplicity, let's assume that your fixed expenses total $2000. That means $2000 would transfer from the Holding Account to your Fixed Account either on the first of the month (ideally) or as you get paid (as discussed in the previous chapter).

Since this expense amount is "fixed," you assign your bank to automatically transfer this same amount every single month from the Holding Account to the Fixed Account.

Then, you have your bank's software pay each of those bills automatically and on time from the Fixed Account. Similarly, you could also have the companies to which you owe the payment auto-draft the payment every month from the Fixed Account. Either way works. I do a little of both.

It's likely the safest plan to have the company for which you owe the payment debit your account. There is less room for error, and it happens electronically. If you decide to make the payment through your bank's bill pay software, there are a couple of things to think about.

For bills owed to larger companies, your bank likely has an electronic relationship with that company. This means that the payments are electronic, and if you schedule them a few days before the deadline, there will be plenty of time for the payment to arrive and be posted.

To make allowances for holidays and weekends, the software will ask you if you want the invoice paid earlier than the payment date you selected or after the payment date you selected if that payment date lands on a holiday or weekend. Take that into your thinking to ensure on-time payment.

Let's look at another example together to help this make sense.

Let's again say your monthly fixed expenses equal $2000. Of that, your house payment is $1400 per month and is due on the 17th, and your car payment is $600 per month and due on the 25th.

On the first of the month, you would have your Holding account transfer $2000 into the Fixed Account. Then, you would have your bank's bill pay software pay your mortgage bill or have your mortgage company deduct the $1,400 mortgage payment automatically prior to the 17th.

If the mortgage company is debiting the account, their software will usually suggest a date to set up the payment to ensure it arrives on time. If you have your bank's bill pay make the payment, then make sure to allow enough time for the payment to arrive and post to the account.

As mentioned earlier, if your bank has an electronic relationship with the mortgage company, then a few days ahead is all that is required.

If your bank doesn't have an electronic relationship with the mortgage company, this means the bank is mailing a physical check. Pay close attention to how long it will take for it to arrive and be processed. Your bank's software will normally tell you when it will arrive.

Remember, this is an actual check, so it must arrive, and someone on the mortgage company's end must actually open it and post it to the account.

In short, electronic is best. Of course, you should simply repeat the process with your $600 car payment.

Now, two of your fixed expenses, which you already pay every month, are paid automatically, and the $2000 is in no danger of being spent by someone in the family overusing the debit card or overspending on Amazon. Why? Because there is no debit card attached to this account.

This account is out of the spending loop. So, we never again have to worry about our fixed expenses not being paid on time every month! Talk about peace of mind!

Most banks provide these services free of charge. They even pay the postage to mail the check. If your bank charges for any of this, then it is probably time to get a new bank.

I want to be very clear about this, so let's look at another example. Let's say your kids are in daycare. The daycare is small; maybe a local church or maybe even a stay-at-home mom that keeps a few kids.

If the amount you pay for daycare is fixed and occurs at a regular interval, you should pay it from the Fixed Account and set it up so that the daycare provider automatically gets a check from your bank every month at the same time.

It does not matter if they are small or local or even an individual. Your bank can send them a check automatically as it would anyone else. Now, that is one less thing for you to worry about.

Remember how I said that having the money transfer on the 1st day of the month is ideal? Let's discuss the process of creating an automatic recurring transfer on the ideal 1st day of the month.

Using the $2000 worth of fixed expenses from the example above, you would log into your online banking and set up an automatic transfer of $2000 to occur on the 1st day of every month from the Holding Account to the Fixed Account with no end date.

Then, you would set up your mortgage company or your bank's bill pay software to pay the mortgage. Then, repeat that process for the car payment.

This means that from now on, $2000 will transfer automatically to the Fixed Account, and the Fixed Account will automatically pay those fixed expenses.

If your expenses never change, you will never have to worry about them again. Of course, things will change over time (you will pay the car off), but not as much or as often as you might think.

When things change, you can change the dollar amount or the timing of the payment. Done!

Now, how does this work if you are paid every two weeks and you are not able to save a whole month's work of expenses in the Holding Account waiting for the first of the month just yet?

This takes a little more strategy and planning. In other words, when you get paid, you have to put that money to work immediately! Hey, I've been there. That is okay; you'll get there.

Let's use that $2,000 number again. Let's assume you get paid on the 1st and 15th of every month. Your mortgage of $1,400 is due on the 10th, and your other fixed expense (car payment) equaling $600 is due on the 25th.

In this example, your first paycheck would still go into the Holding Account on the 1st of the month. On the 2nd of the month, you would create an automatic transfer from the Holding Account to the Fixed Account for $1400. The Fixed Account would automatically pay the mortgage due on the 10th.

Then, when you are paid on the 15th, you will create an automatic transfer on the 16th from the Holding Account to the Fixed Account for $600. The Fixed Account would then automatically pay the car payment due on the 25th. Again, all of this should be set up to occur automatically.

Whew! I know that was a lot to take in, so let's quickly review so you do not get discouraged or lose focus. In its simplest form, remember this is all that is happening.

You have fixed expenses every month or expenses that do not regularly change. These expenses include things like your mortgage and maybe car payments.

You will set up a Fixed Account to pay those expenses automatically. This means you no longer worry about whether you have paid the most important expenses you have every month.

You may not believe this, but my mortgage payment never crosses my mind. My Fixed Account pays that mortgage on time every month.

Maybe you want to give $500 to your church every month. That $500 would go into the Fixed Account and then automatically be paid out to your church via bank check or, if your church is technologically advanced, via automatic fund transfer (ACH).

You could even decide to invest $500 each month toward your retirement or other investments. This would also be transferred into the Fixed Account and then automatically transferred to your investment.

Using this system to save for investing automatically means you do not have to make the decision every month about whether you have money left to invest (or save).

You have committed to doing it by setting it up to happen automatically, and you are actually doing it without thinking about it. You are paying yourself FIRST! Bam! Trust me, you are going to love this.

Helpful Tip: Remember, if you currently have fixed expenses auto-drafted from any of your other bank accounts, you will want to re-direct those to this account.

CHAPTER 4

IRREGULAR EXPENSES ACCOUNT
YES DEBIT CARD ACCOUNT

The Irregular Expenses Account is a holding place for expenses that we know are going to occur. However, they either do not occur at regular intervals or the dollar amount of the expense is not fixed.

The purpose of this account is to ensure you have money set aside for those expenses because they are coming!

Much like the Fixed Account, we want these dollars set aside and removed from our day-to-day spending.

This account is going to give you so many wonderful moments of, "Oh no, the alternator went out on the car! Wait, we have been putting money aside for that every month. Ok cool, fix the car. No worries!"

That is exactly how I feel and react every single time, even to this day, when an unplanned but inevitable expense occurs. You may ask, "If it is unplanned, doesn't that make it an emergency?"

No. We know these things are going to happen we do not know the date and time. It is like keeping an umbrella in your car. We know eventually, rain will come.

We do not know the very moment it will start to rain but we plan for it by keeping an umbrella handy.

When will your car's brakes go out? When will the tires wear out? When might an alternator go out? We do not have a fixed date for these expenses, and we do not have a fixed dollar amount for them, so how in the world do we plan for them?

First things first, we know these things are going to happen. We know cars break down and houses need repair. So, if we know these things are going to happen, we need a plan for them. However, we do not have to have some major algebraic equation and an actuarial chart to create a strategy.

What are some other things that might fit into the Irregular Expenses Account?

How about events we know are coming, like birthdays, Christmas, graduation, etc.? Listen. You know you are going to get those kids something for Christmas this year—you are.

So why are we surprised when we wake up the Friday after Thanksgiving and say, "HOLY SMOKES! Christmas is just around the corner! How are we going to buy gifts?" Christmas is the same time every single year. We can do better than this. Here is how.

The way I manage this account is simple to understand but takes a little time to prepare.

Here is a list of some irregular expenses that are common:

- Birthdays
- Anniversaries
- Medical Expenses
- Dental Expenses
- Auto Repairs
- Christmas/Holidays
- Home Repairs
- Back to School Shopping
- Seasonal Clothes for Kids
- Kid's Sports or Activity Dues
- Vacation/Travel

Now, I want you to create a list of things you have paid for over the last 12 months, like I did above. Make sure to exclude fixed expenses and normal living expenses like food, gas, or household items.

Second, go to your handy computer and print off every bank statement or credit card statement from the last 12 months. It does not matter if you do a calendar year (Jan. – Dec.) or start with your current month and look back 12 months.

Now, take a highlighter and highlight anything that you feel falls within the list of categories that you made. No need to keep each category separated.

We are going to pay these out of one account. Now that you have highlighted them-add them all up. This number may shock you a little and can be a little scary. I'll bet you had no idea you paid that much for those kinds of things!

Now, let's do a little division. Take that big number and divide it by 12. Let's say that number equaled $3600. If we divide that by 12, we get $300.

This means that every month, the Holding Account will transfer $300 into the Irregular Expenses Account. When one of the above things occurs, you won't have to worry. Just take your checkbook for this account or debit card and pay it.

If you use this account for birthdays, Christmas, or vacations, keep a list of how much you allocated for those types of things. For example, if you allocated $50 per month for Christmas, then $600 is about what you would want to spend on Christmas out of this account.

If having debit card access to this money is too tempting, restrict access to this account. Choose not to have a debit card. How would that work?

When an expense arises that falls into the Irregular Expenses Account category, determine how much you will need to cover it, and then transfer just that amount from the Irregular Expenses Account into your Everyday Expenses Account (we will discuss the Everyday Expenses Account in the next chapter).

Then, use your Everyday Expenses Account debit card to pay the expense. This puts a step between you and a bad-moment spending decision with your Irregular Expenses dollars.

It forces you to go into your account and transfer the money. That gives you time to think before you whip out your Irregular Expenses debit card and pay for something you do not need.

This Irregular Expenses Account will always be a work in progress. You will never get it exactly right down to the dollar.

In the beginning, you could put $300 there in the first month for car repair, and sure enough, the car breaks down in the first month, and the cost is $500. That is okay; that is life. Once you get it going, things will normalize over time.

If you end a calendar year with too much money in the account, then adjust and fund a little less in the coming year. What if you run out of money in this account? You will need to invest a few more dollars in there every month.

So, how do you manage if your car and home repairs cost more this year than you had deposited into the Irregular Expenses Account? Great question!

It could be that the gifts you give this year are less expensive. Maybe you will have to work a little overtime. You might even have to pull a little from the Everyday Expenses Account.

The important thing is that you assign a reasonable dollar amount to this account every single month. We know these expenses are coming, and we do not want to put them on a credit card or borrow from parents or someone else.

This account will create tremendous peace in your life. You can do this! Let's examine the plan we have built up to this point by looking at an example.

EXAMPLE PLAN

Let's take a $8,000-a-month salary and walk through the process. Here is our example budget.

INCOME = $8000

FIXED EXPENSES:		IRREGULAR EXPENSES:	
House	$1000	Car Repairs	$200
Cars	$800	Home Repairs	$200
Giving	$800	Medical Expenses	$250
Investing	$800	Dental Expense	$100
Car Insurance	$200	Vet	$50
Life Insurance	$400		
Total	$4000	Total	$800

Let's start with January. For the entire month of January, our income of $8,000 has been deposited into the Holding Account waiting for the first of the month. On February 1, we set up the Holding Account to transfer $4000 into the Fixed Account to cover all fixed expenses.

On February 1, we set up the Holding Account to transfer $800 to the Irregular Expenses Account to cover irregular expenses.

That leaves us with $3200. On Feb 1st, we will have the Holding Account transfer $3200 automatically into our Everyday Expenses Account (next chapter).

If everything stays the same, from that month forward all these amounts will transfer to each of the accounts automatically.

The Fixed Account will pay all our fixed expenses automatically.

The Irregular Expenses Account will hold funds until one of the irregular expenses we have been saving for occurs.

> **Helpful Tip:** Since you will have multiple debit cards in your wallet/purse, make sure you write the name of each account on your debit card for you and your partner.

CHAPTER 5

EVERYDAY EXPENSES ACCOUNT
YES, DEBIT CARD

That gets us to the Everyday Expenses Account, where you will do all your day-to-day spending.

This will be for food, fuel, clothes, oil changes, utilities like gas and water and any other spur-of-the-moment goodies you can afford.

This account is where the Holding Account will transfer most of what is left of your salaries after you have funded the Fixed Expenses Account and Irregular Expenses Accounts. The Everyday Expenses Account is for your day-to-day living expenses.

Before we move on, let's make sure to make a mental note of where you are in simple terms. We have already automatically made our money do many of the most important things it was supposed to do! What does that mean? It means we have set up our Fixed Expenses Account and our Irregular Expenses Account to handle the big financial obligations in our life.

It means we are financially awesome, and we are being great stewards of what God has given us. We are not flying by the seat of our pants any longer.

We have a plan. Sure, this plan basically runs itself. Sure, it feels like doing good ought to be harder than this, but it is not! This means a percentage of our remaining dollars is discretionary to some degree. How does that feel? Good, right?!

I know, I know. You still need to eat, you still need to fill up the car, and you may need a few clothes, but in most cases, we have some discretion over how much we spend. For example, if your income is a little lower this month, avoid eating out, make sandwiches at home, and eliminate driving unless it is necessary.

You can decide to keep wearing your old clothes for a while longer (these clothes are not old; they are vintage), or you can buy the clothes you must have from the thrift store. That's right! It will not kill you. I promise. The bottom line is that everyone has choices in areas like these.

Let's use our numbers from the previous chapter. As in the previous chapter let's assume that in January, we have been depositing all our income into the Holding Account ($8,000).

We have already discussed the Fixed Expenses Account gets $4,000 and the Irregular Expenses Account gets $800. Leaving $3,200 for the Everyday Expenses Account.

On Feb 1, the Holding Account will deposit $3,200 into the Everyday Expenses Account. We will use this money all month to run our household.

Once that is set up, all that is left to do is manage the money in the Everyday Expenses Account. This is easily done by dividing the money in this account by the number of days left in the month, or you could also divide it by four weeks.

On the first day of the month, if you have $3,200 in the Everyday Expenses account, this means you can spend around $800 per week.

Or get more granular with a daily calculation. Let's imagine that it is now the 20th of the month, and there is $1,500 left in the Everyday Expenses account. That leaves you roughly 10 days left in the month. Quick math will tell you that if you divide $1,500 by 10 days, you have $150 per day that you can spend. It is that easy!

You do not need fancy budgeting spreadsheets or software. Lock in the total dollars in this account and manage your spending with simple mind math.

For the Everyday Expenses Account, it is imperative to have bank account visibility on your mobile phone. You and your partner need always to know how much is in this account.

If you think having a month's worth of dollars in the Everyday Expenses account at one time is too much of a temptation, do it this way.

Let's say you have determined that $3,200 will go into this account every month. For easy math, let's go with a four-week month. You could have your Holding Account transfer $800 on the 1st, $800 on the 8th, $800 on the 15th and $800 on the 22nd automatically or at whatever interval you choose.

This will prevent you from spending the entire budget for this account in the first week. Look at you—you are budgeting without even trying!

In our household, we transfer the entire amount on the first day of the month and manage the dollars as the month progresses. Some months, we spend too much in week one, which means we must be more careful in weeks two through four.

If we are not careful, we may run out of money. But remember, even if you spend too much in week one, you have not risked your house or car payment.

You are only working with money that has very little risk attached to it. In most (not all) American households, I'd be willing to bet that if you could not buy food for one week, you would not starve.

There are enough cans of beans, ramen noodles, and tuna in the pantry, not to mention the food in the freezer you have not looked at in two years. If you do not have that type of reserve, then you will have to be more careful with these dollars.

The bottom line is that you will learn to manage these dollars and work it out week by week. Even in our household, by the fourth week, we are ready to get paid again.

We run this account low every single month. Should I feel bad about that? No!

I have already done all the good I wanted to do in my other accounts. There is no condemnation and nothing to feel guilty about. Spend it all every month if you want!

This account does require communication, trust, and partnership. If you are married or sharing accounts/spending with someone else, you will need to work together. Both parties will always need instant and total visibility of this account on their phones.

Both parties involved must know how much is in this account to manage the spending properly. Also, remember, any large or irregular purchases that would take the account down below where it would need to be to finish out the month easily need to be discussed before the purchase.

This account is a great marriage builder; it requires communication!

How does it feel to be free? Amazing!

Also, make sure you know your bank's minimum account balance and endeavor not to go below that. This minimum account balance should be something very low, like $50 or $10. If your bank's minimum account balance requirement is more than that, it is time to change banks.

> **Helpful Tip:** Do not forget to label your debit cards for you and your partner. Literally, write Everyday Expenses on your debit card.

CHAPTER 6

FREEDOM ACCOUNTS
YES, DEBIT CARD

You have made it! All the hard work is over. You have made it to a fun time! Everybody needs a little money to blow.

Men, women and old financial misers like me need a little bit of money to spend however we want with zero guilt and no judgement.

That is where the Freedom Accounts come to the rescue. In these accounts, each partner will get their own spending money to do with what they want with ZERO guilt or judgement.

If you are single and the household is just you, then you still need to set up a Freedom Account. For some of you, these may not even be accounts yet. You may pull this amount in cash, but the important thing is to have some dollars individually that each partner has complete control over.

These dollars are not to be saved for household expenses or emergencies. They are to be spent as the account owner desires. For some of you, that may be $10 per month, and for some of you, that may be a much larger amount. The important thing is that it happens and it works within your budget. How each person spends those dollars is completely up to that person. No judgments!

If you decide to set up bank accounts for your Freedom spending, do so just like the others and have your Holding Account deposit the agreed-upon amounts into these accounts on the 1st of every month.

Here is my real-world example. After setting up all our accounts, my lovely wife Vanessa and I decided together how much to put into her Freedom Account each month. Those dollars are her dollars.

I no longer have any say whatsoever over how she spends those dollars. She can save them over several months and buy something big, or she can spend every penny every month.

She can buy shoes and more shoes. She can literally roll the car window down and toss those dollars out the window. Are you ready to hear what my response will be no matter what she does with the money?

My job is to be her cheerleader! "Wow, Babe! Nobody throws money out the window as well as you do! You are amazing!" Obviously, that scenario is ridiculous, but it does make my point.

There is nothing she can do with that money that I don't applaud. It is hers to enjoy. Likewise, the money in my Freedom Account is the same.

I challenge any of you who know our family to ask my wife if I have ever questioned, even one time, what she has spent out of her Freedom Account. She will smile and tell you I have not. She loves it.

Do not skip these accounts; they are important. Look each other in the eye and, with grace, work toward determining the correct amount. **These accounts are relationship enhancers!**

CHAPTER 7

THE HOW-TO

LET'S GET YOU SET UP.

To begin with, we have to create our one-time starter budget. This is not a difficult process. Remember, you are only going to do this once—or maybe once a year!

1ST

Determine your fixed expenses: house payment, car payment, and anything that has a fixed amount and a fixed due date. Don't be anxious about overlooking a fixed expense during this first pass. If you miss one, you will recognize it later, and then you can add it to the Fixed Account at that time.

2ND

Determine what your Irregular Expenses are. This is a little more time-consuming, but not difficult.

A. Make a list of your irregular expenses in the previous year. These could include things like car repair, home repair, doctor's visits, and dental costs. You could even add in vacation, Christmas, and possibly clothes for the kids' new school year. These are expenses that you know are coming, but you do not know when or how much.

B. Now print out your previous year's bank statements. Go through each line, looking for items that are on your list. For example, car repair should likely be an expected expense for your Irregular Expenses account. Go through last year's bank statements and note every dollar you spent on car repair. Let's imagine you spent $1,200 last year. Divide that number by 12 ($100); now you know you will need to deposit $100 for car repair into your Irregular Expenses account each month. Do this for all the items on the Irregular Expenses list that you created.

C. Now, total all of those up and divide by 12. This is the amount you need to fund your Irregular Expenses account. It will never be perfect. We are not looking for perfection, just progress, and we do not want to borrow money for these things when they occur.

3RD

After doing the above two exercises, you are getting closer to knowing your monthly needs. So, let's go back to our bank statements again and look at what living necessities we have missed. We must eat, and we must put gas in the car. The number we are searching for here is what it takes monthly to meet your basic needs. This number is the minimum amount required to run your household.

This is an important number to know, especially if your income each month is not fixed. For example, if you need $5000 each month to pay for everything, eat and put gas in the car, and if your salary over each year averages $5000 per month, but some months it is $4000, and some months it is $6000, that will let you know how much to tell the Holding Account to disburse to the other accounts each month.

Or, once we know this number and realise that we are making more than it takes to meet our basic needs, we can decide what our accounts should do with the excess.

Do we want to invest and save? Do we want to spend a little more and maybe go on another vacation? Do we want to give more?

We cannot make a good decision about these things until we know our number. I realize doing these first three steps is not a ton of fun, but this system allows you to do it once, or at most once a year and then it becomes automated!

4TH

Now that we have an amount for steps 1, 2, and 3, we can decide what amounts should go into our Everyday Expenses and Freedom Accounts. You will have to work closely with your significant other to determine the right amount for each of your Freedom Accounts.

Remember, the two Freedom Accounts do not have to be bank accounts, you could choose to get cash for this.

After the Freedom Account amounts have been determined, whatever is left can go into your

Everyday Expenses Account; this is what you will live off day-to-day. And remember, you can spend this account down to almost zero every month without guilt.

Why? Because you have done all the good things.

Now, here is a little tip from me. It is important to save and invest for your future. So, push yourself to do a good job of saving and investing.

A great rule of thumb is to live off 70% of your income and use the remaining 30% to invest in your future. That would also include getting out of bad consumer debt, like credit card debt.

5TH

Although I strongly encourage you to follow steps 1-4, if you really do not feel like you can do all the above steps, then do this.

- A. Start with step 1. Determine your fixed expenses and make a list of them. Determine the exact dollar amount for those expenses each month.

- B. Assign a number to the Irregular Expenses Account; depending on your income/expenses, this could be $50 per month, $5000 per month or any number you choose.

C. As you work through the system month to month, adjust the amounts going into the Fixed and Irregular Expenses accounts over time until you get it nailed down. This will allow you to work the system and adjust along the way until you get it right. It is not the preferred method, but it is still effective.

OPENING ACCOUNTS

Most of you already have accounts open at your bank that you can rename and then assign one of the jobs mentioned earlier in the book. Remember that it is imperative that all parties utilizing these bank accounts have electronic access on phone and/or computer.

There are two ways to get the appropriate accounts open.

1. Do it all online. This is how I did mine. I logged into my bank website and opened all the accounts. Then, it is very important to nickname them Fixed, Irregular, Everyday Expenses, and Freedom Account(s).

For the Freedom accounts, it is typically Her Freedom and His Freedom, or you can use your names. For us, it was Eric Freedom and Vanessa Freedom. Nicknaming the accounts makes it easier to look at them on your computer or phone and set up transfers. It is critical to your success.

You may not think it is that important because you know what the accounts are. However, generally, there is one spouse or one member of the relationship that is less involved. If the nicknames are clear and they understand the process, it will be simpler and more palatable for them.

You will also choose which accounts you want checks and debit cards for. Remember that not all of them will have checks or debit cards. Before you are able to start using the system completely, you will have to wait until your debit cards are mailed to your house

.

2. If you do not feel you can set the accounts up yourself online, then take your list of accounts to your bank. Remember to make an appointment,

and you will likely need to plan to have your spouse go with you.

It will probably take a couple of hours to open and set up all these accounts. As in the paragraph above, make sure you can nickname the accounts and let the banker know if you want checks or debit cards.

Also, if you are not familiar with the bank's software, they may be able to show you how to use that too. Once your debit cards come in, you may have to go back to the bank to have them help you set up the fund transfers if you are not comfortable working with the software.

I will stop and say here that if you are not comfortable working with online banking, this system will be more challenging for you. Because every time you need to change something, you will need to go to the bank. Take the time to get comfortable with online banking. You will be glad you did.

3. Once your debit cards are in, now you are ready to get the automation going.

HOLDING ACCOUNT – NO DEBIT CARD

This is where you will have to discuss with your HR department or with whoever is paying you that you have a new account to have your check direct deposited into or to have your business that you own pay your salary into this account.

Remember, all personal income comes into this account first. Then, on the first day of the month, we will have it disburse funds into the other accounts. Remember to set the transfers up as recurring.

FIXED EXPENSES ACCOUNT – NO DEBIT CARD

At this point, you should know your fixed expenses. On the First Day of the month, have the Holding account deposit the exact amount into the Fixed Expenses Account to cover those expenses, even if some of them are annual fixed expenses.

Then, go into your bank's software and schedule automatic payment of all your fixed expenses. Take each invoice or coupon for the fixed expenses due and set up an automatic bill payment from this account.

Remember, if you use the Bank's Bill Pay and they do not have an electronic relationship with the vendor, then the bank will mail a physical check. Allow time for this to happen.

For example, if your due date is on the 12th and you know the bank is going to have to send a check, then you should have your bank send the check on the 2nd. Your bank's software will tell you when the check will arrive or, if electronic, when the payment will arrive.

Remember, you can also have the company that you owe automatically debit the account rather than have the bank pay it.

> **Helpful Tip:** Since the money comes into this account on the 1st, I would not have any bills paid on the 1st; I would start at least on the 2nd.

As mentioned, I would not run any account down to zero every month. Instead, determine your bank's minimum account balance, if it has one.

If your bank has a minimum account balance, endeavor not to go below that amount. If your bank does not have a minimum account balance, set one for yourself. For example, if the number was $50, then every month, this account would get down to $50. That is okay; that is exactly what is supposed to happen.

IRREGULAR EXPENSES – DEBIT CARD MAYBE

At this point, you should know what your irregular expenses are. On the First Day of the month, have the Holding account deposit the amount into the Irregular Expenses account to cover those expenses. Remember to make it recurring.

As those expenses that you listed as irregular expenses occur, pay them from this account. Also, let's say that you have included things like vacation, Christmas, and fun things like this into this account. Make a note of how much you are depositing for those types of things.

For example, let's say you deposit $100 per month for things like Christmas and Vacation. However, you also deposit $100 per month for your other irregular expenses, for a total of $200 per month.

When it is time to take a vacation, and you have $2400 in this account, that does not mean you have money for a $2400 vacation. Only use your agreed-upon amount for the fun things. You'll need your other deposits to cover other expenses.

As mentioned, I would not run any account down to zero every month, so put $50 or so in there (or whatever the bank's minimum account balance is), and that would always be the low watermark.

FREEDOM ACCOUNTS - YES DEBIT CARD

By this time, you and your partner will have decided the amount that you are going to put into your Freedom Accounts (if you decide to use accounts instead of cash). On the first day of the month, the Holding Account transfers those amounts into the Freedom Accounts. Remember to make it recurring.

EVERYDAY EXPENSES - YES DEBIT CARD

At this point, you should know how much it takes to run your monthly budget, so after subtracting the Fixed, Irregular, and Freedom account values, on the first day of the month, have the Holding Account transfer the difference between those numbers and your monthly budget amount into the Everyday Expenses Account.

Or, as discussed earlier, if you cannot trust yourself with a whole month's worth of money, have the Holding Account break that month's worth of funding up to 2 transfers or 4 transfers into the Everyday Expenses.

CHAPTER 8

EMERGENCY FUND
NO DEBIT CARD

Let me touch on an account that I have not mentioned in this book: the Emergency Fund. This is a savings account and this account is critical to your financial success!

Life happens, and at some point, something completely unexpected and impossible to plan for is going to occur. That is why we have the Emergency Fund.

It is important to have access to this money, but not easy to access. I recommend you open this account in another bank, or you could use part of the cash value from a Life Insurance policy as your Emergency Fund.

Set up this account so that you have limited access. You may want to consider setting it up so that you must physically go to the bank to get this money if you need it.

Why? Because if it is too easy to get to, then it is too easy to get to.

Most of us will lie to ourselves and say, "I'll borrow a little from the Emergency Fund this month, and I will pay it back next month." My friend, that never works! So, put an obstacle between you and these dollars.

What constitutes an "emergency?" An emergency is job loss, or perhaps the water heater explodes in your house, and you need to pay someone immediately to clean up the mess before the insurance company can get you a check. These are emergencies.

Things like kids' braces, tires, brakes, and gifts are not emergencies. Why? Because we already know these things are coming.

Forgetting your sister's birthday yesterday is not an emergency. It is the same day since she was born. We have been planning for these events in your other accounts. These events are important, but they are not emergencies.

You may be wondering, "How much should I have in my Emergency Fund?" Great question.

Most experts agree that savings equal to 3–6 months of expenses should be enough. Do not panic if that seems like an impossibility. Let's start small.

Make a goal to put $500 into your Emergency Fund as quickly as possible. Make some sacrifices or have a yard sale. Just do whatever you can to put that buffer between you and life.

Try never to spend that money. Work hard to build it up to the target amount of 3-6 months' worth of expenses. You can do this.

Nothing worth doing is ever going to be easy. All worthwhile endeavours are uphill. This is not too big for you. It's not nothing but a step for a stepper!

CHAPTER 9

PAYING YOURSELF FIRST

INVEST IN YOURSELF

In Chapter 3, I briefly mentioned using the Fixed Account to transfer dollars automatically for investing purposes. Some people call this "Paying Yourself First."

Many of us have had conversations with ourselves and maybe our spouses about starting to save. "We will save next month. We will save whatever is left over in the checking account at the end of the month."

The problem is there is almost never anything left over. That is because our spending will always rise to the level of our income.

For many of us, our spending rises to a level greater than our income. So, if we can agree that saving for the future or saving to fund an investment to get closer to our goals is a noble pursuit, then we need a better plan.

The better plan is to automate your saving/investing to occur at the beginning of the month or as soon as you get paid.

Have those savings accumulate in an account that is outside of your normal monthly spending accounts. This is critical to getting ahead and reaching your goals.

Ultimately, most of us want to work less in the near term so we can spend more time with the people that matter. Or maybe we want to have a stable retirement income so that we can pursue our interests without debilitating budget constraints.

Unless you have a big inheritance in your future or you were born independently wealthy, the only way to do this is to have your money working for you instead of you working for your money.

Currently, I am working closely with Wealth Without Wall Street, which has a podcast by the same name. Their passion is helping people find ways to create

Passive Income and teaching them how to achieve financial freedom. I'm a big believer in the Infinite Banking Concept, which is the process of becoming your own bank, but that's for another book. If you have questions about that, please reach out to me from the YourAutomatedBudget.com website.

WHAT IS FINANCIAL FREEDOM?

Financial freedom is when your Passive Income is greater than your monthly expenses. If you are entrepreneurial at all or have ever considered starting a side hustle, this podcast deserves a listen.

If that is not you and you are content working for someone else in a W2-type position, that is ok, too. Not everyone is cut out to run their own business or do a side hustle. One way to automate savings in a W2 situation is to payroll deduct your investment dollars.

Most companies offer a retirement plan in the form of a 401k or 403b, or you can invest independently in an IRA. While I believe there are better vehicles for financial freedom than the traditional 401k/IRA route, I believe the most important thing is to get your money working for you.

In summary, pay yourself first, right off the top, into an investment vehicle or side hustle of some kind. Or, if you are an evangelical Christian and a tither, pay your tithes first, then pay yourself second.

Doing this and putting your money to work for you is the fastest way to financial freedom.

Here is the most important investment you can make: invest in your financial education. You are doing this right now. Continue to pursue knowledge. You will grow, and you will find the answers.

CHAPTER 10

THE WRAP-UP

DO THE WORK. LIVE WELL.

People who do well with their money do not do well by accident. You must do something. You must make something happen.

Yes, doing a written budget every month is the very best way to manage your money. However, if you cannot or won't stick with a budget—it isn't very helpful.

You need to find a money management system you can or will do. I believe this plan to automate all your financial transactions is the second-best way to manage your money. It can become the very best way if it is one you will use.

I am proud of you for reading this book. What this tells me is that you are a person who is serious about taking control of your finances.

You are so much further ahead than almost everyone around you. Do not stop here. Push. Find people whose natural behaviour matches your goal behaviour. Then, start spending time with them.

When you do this, you level UP! If your goal is to run a marathon, you cannot spend your days training with people who walk two miles a day. You have got to spend time with the marathoners!

Even if you can only run part of the way with them, to begin with, before long, their passion, experience, and tenacity will rub off on you! Then, you will become a marathoner, too. The same is true for finances or any other behaviour you want to emulate!

If you are single, go for it! If you are married, get your partner to join you, and work together to change your family's future. Teach others.

Remember, you have got this!

www.ingramcontent.com/pod-product-compliance
Lightning Source LLC
Chambersburg PA
CBHW071841210526
45479CB00001B/241